but first I call your name

Hadassa Tal

but first I call your name

*translated from Hebrew
by Joanna Chen*

Shearsman Books

First published in the United Kingdom in 2021 by
Shearsman Books Ltd
PO Box 4239
Swindon
SN3 9FN

Shearsman Books Ltd Registered Office
30–31 St. James Place, Mangotsfield, Bristol BS16 9JB
(this address not for correspondence)

www.shearsman.com

ISBN 978-1-84861-779-7

But first I call your name was first published in Israel by
Hakibbutz Hameuchad-Sifriat Poalim Publishing Group, 2017.

Cover design: Elad Naftali
With thanks to Amon Yariv, Gordon Gallery.

With special thanks to Julia AK

Contents

* *

for Maya

within the whirlpool of your loss
I'm a reflection
this pearl of light
that falls
is you
apart from everything
nothing has changed

maybe

I will discover your name
will shout it, shout slowly
maybe breathe
be silent
maybe
blend it with a select variety of grape,
slurp it down, roaring and moist of spirit.
Maybe I will whisper a psalm to the seaweed
will suck it out of rocks sweating in the light,
legs dangling in water.
Maybe I will rip out the silence
seal it in the belly of a cicada,
and from the landslide of its voice
your name will rise utterly human,
filling life with sweetness.
Maybe I will ply the rose with passion
sprout grief in the soil
and with the flightiness of spring
it might flower
and out of the shudders of an unpruned garden
I'll lip
come
it's dinnertime –
just speak to me, speak like the seasons,
speak to me like rain,
speak
maybe then I will know the immortal song of mortals.

crumbs

With a scarf, because it grows cold at dusk,
especially on the beach,
dress unbuttoned, held by a moon-shaped pin
precisely in the middle of the chest
raising arms, exposing them to seagulls,
slipping away between piers running along stone platforms
chasing you

The water resting as the morning star and a girl fall,
scattering through the air

you slipped

like silk
over skin
naked body –
breast of night
burning
star

how much yearning does time weigh?

You yearn from within me
passing a shadow over my words, pushing
toward the source of light.
On a page of the universe your face rests
softly twirling the world around

You've been emptied of clocks yet time happens
dangling the world from a thread
a night and seven days and always
the unknown depths
and emptiness
filled with itself

* *

Oh days of innocence under dazzling sun
once I loaned a lupine from the bees

rainy days are good for onions, you laughed

Our ancestors likened it to a large pearl,
the French turned it into soup.
You cannot taste it without tears.

You laughed,
a laugh removed from language,
your spirit rebelling
wandering along in the opposite direction
to laughter

santa rosa

With which word, which silence can I say: No. Pain
is nailed, flowing outside of time.
Gathering all the no mores –
no more inhaling dandelions,
no more plums blushing at lunch,
no more winter chestnuts on the palate.
We bit into them at night, we bit and bit each time
the bats flew south
reverberating

lacuna

I want to lure you with words impossible
to hunt, translate or plunder.
This morning I listened to hushed tones, and then
a word, I swear, began singing –
if only it would sprout feathers
you'd never know the difference
except for
the comma –
take it, it's yours, only promise me
don't pause

echo

Bottles freeze behind the milky blindness
of glass. Silence. No murmur.
I know how it guzzles words
chilled by the warmth of its breath,
how it rages and goes.
I never dreamed
you would

the last bucket

more than the crepe, muslin and chiffon of castles,
the king loves tea. leaning on a moon-hoof of delicate silver,
heaven perched beneath his ankles, he dribbles into the last
bucket of black elderberry tea.
below, at the corner of coronation street where clocks gather,
there's a clock for every second of His wild years.
time moves away from its pitchers when the lusterless king yawns:
humpty dumpty sat on a wall,
humpty dumpty had a
great fall

* *

I know I dreamt it. we crept
into the backyard of his locked sleep
the two of us dancing
dust

…& all the king's horses & all the king's men
couldn't put humpty together again

your body repels

There's no need to wear white
your beauty imbibed
the words left
behind,
discarded
like clothing, and
this is just you
with
nothing

* *

The saddest of lemon trees springs from tears
on a leaf of paper a songbird
blinds letters that dance her to the bough-tip
all is you, crushing the silence.

said the moon

I come like the lonely the maddened the muddled
stirring a swarm in the water's reflection.
Doubts are already being dragged into ocean,
everything blows at the whim of a wind

silence

When he heard his own words, Time looked up, startled.
Nevermore, he said, Nevermore
and then silence split in two.
Pythia heard too, unraveling an answer, so indistinct.
Autumn fell and a strange rustling erupted. In spring,
she promised, there'll be soft tidings and
a flower will tell you its name. And in winter?
Rain lashing a willow branch will be the only tune,
the world tethered to these words: you are no

that's that

how can I say it?
(this darkness on each eyelid)
a voice jingles
in a bell
polished by the void

sanctified

by
ruling
Mekudeshet
Mekudeshet
Mekudeshet
eternity
made
you
its
own

run away
leave the poem

* *

i run barefoot along a strip of sand,
under an umbrella of cloud.
the seven lakes speak tears that hide you

leave these words

Night lives within them, pale eyed.
Deep into the music they shoot you a look,
shoot with precision,
playing on birds and dreams.
Inertia spills into pools of light ruptured by lightning,
freckles appear on your face, your breasts,
the dress that clings to your body.
Rain begins falling, hailstones hurl down,
if only a moon floated on the heart of night
at night at night,
floating yellowy,
if only it wept

Leave these words
an inevitable shuddering, vitreous cracks
do not reveal the fragments within
don't you get it?
And I run, run like a broom through the city streets,
my hands a dustpan for tears, a vessel for weeping,

everything is a horizon
withdrawing into dreams
Pompeii of the soul.

Was it my yearning that created the rose you gave me
in a dream or was it yours –

Look at you
you who are like no other
are now like the earth.

The earth?
couldn't be –
sand clings to my lips like trepidation.

Misfortune conceals a distant equation of beauty,
turns weeds green, sweeps red on the lips of a rose,
the pistil stands tall, licked by tongues of wind.
A squill too large to bear
blooms above the depth that covers itself
with your name.
Painfully terrified, refusing
the no-light, the non-fire,

you are held tight while a bird,
gazes blankly as fortuity moans.

Everything speaks
. yet silence is unbroken.
I hover whispering incantation
reaching out
to the aerial roots of ancient verses
running to capture the soul and plant it here.
Stay here, it is here you belong, oh stay,
stay in the breast
the womb

leave these words
run away
at any moment quiet will ring out from the bells
leave it

        run

* *

grief gripping my temple like a loaded gun

* *

Why. the most ancient assemblage of cadence

one instant – you're gone
I call the fin infinity

aquarelle

Anything else can still be doubted
but the amaranthine velvet circling her head
sun-hot by my side
is endless beautiful. Wounded within a spill of red
gray becomes clouds of dripping water
things flash like fire through fog
birds flee –
only where the sun drowns
the landscape seeps
to sea

handwritten

I know the handwriting of the wind, the prose
that dust collects, free of weight, April's sky
when winds are driven inward,
when clouds hover low over
trees, and feijoa flips from branch to branch,
and black-blushed pitango scribbles verse,
tossed by the wind.
Speak the core of being
speak crude, elusive. Speak without fear,
core within core, speak pearl that is not camellia
but sweet primrose pulling bees to naked petals
blanching in yolky dress,
blue as lavender, daisies entangled in lust.
Speak the core, speak time that lies ahead.
Soon the passiflora clocks will ripen
curling in and as they strike violet
the last lemon will fall.
Leave berries in the branches,
flimsy letters seeping through the page.
Cry the peony whose beauty impedes silence,
wear the pulverized rose with tatters of light,
shout yes yes
and cry some more imbibed by beauty.
I'll recognize the script,
the forest-cradle dangling:
here I am, in two heartbeats – here

cat

Sprawled across a quilt of weeds, leafy bedclothes,
the breasts, softly brazen, babied in pristine vapor.
Below, two pale pink solitary nipples,
a still-warm belly, a gaping navel.
A kitten curls up there, eyelids drooping.
Lips protrude above that canyon
and all's alive up to the freckle,
the hidden plumage.
Ah flesh brimming vitality
Ah beauty all that beauty
How will I commit you to soil

non finito

...the rest is *non finito*
things brought to fruition
without ending...

january 2013

Did I tell you how January flew by breathless,
cloud-stained
a snowstorm clutching its right foot
how the skies nudged it
how the ice frosted over
how
no
fell
with
yes

* *

at that moment I was no more than a plundered wing.
every night besieged by barn owls. imitating death.
and the world encircled it, obeying the power of weakness

guesstimate

they say your loosened curls are the wings of the bird of fate
that you were already who you would be
that you wouldn't have been eternal
if you hadn't been transient

she-dog

mouth erupts in a howl
tormenting
the flesh

the inseparable
ripped
one from the
other

owwww she-dog
stray-dog
seeps through me

* *

stars burn above the dome of thought
the night vine eats her grapes nipple by nipple
returning the power of solace to earth

and then

I swore
every morning to sift death
from the death within

I swore
heart beating
bearing witness

I will not be able to lift you
my love is heavier than words

woman,

in everything else you're a child.
Like the moment before nuptials,
flawless in the middle of a marketplace,
trampling the dirt that sprays up, morphing
into petrifying pitch. The camera ceases
when you sing from on top of a stall, belting out
Björk to a startling beat. The moon
peels down to nipples and honey
as night falls –
first slowly, then sprinting as you scatter flowers,
looping and spiraling, all of you love-struck white
running faster than
beauty

in athens

You captured the Acropolis, the Agora,
the Dionysus Theater, the street's rumble,
idols, fishmongers, flea-fairs.
You said an angel of history leads to us,
standing at the edge.
We talked our life, talked our death

suspended. The most shut – opened.
Space blurs the surface of a snapshot,
the eyes' caves peeping out like gaps in a plot –
only those you left
burning

buongiorno, notte

Way back in Florence, Pepe's kitchen.
Pizza de Pomodoro, fine but not too thin,
plenty of cherry tomatoes fired through with smoke,
the parmesan smooth and honeyed, the dough
airborne, thrown,
caught slightly
charred.
On the floor, trash cradles a bundle of mint,
cans, olives, its belly full of pickings not yet emptied.
The kids alone share chaos, rehearsing
with passion, licking their fingers, unflinching

johann sebastian ugh

I pumped Bach while you picked Bob, kicking the prose
right in the belly of song, wanting wild-rock, some
fresh Dylan on hard ground.
You didn't think much of Bach, even though he beats time
...Johann Sebastian ugh, mamma, you told me

signing with a bite
on the butt of the piano, an old piano
once owned by a bishop
whose name was
lost

blues

In the metro tunnel at St. Paul's, I played
on braids of light,
a prism of musical strings.
In one gulp I improvised colors crashed

blues – quickening me, more,
vibrato more
broken pitch
kicked-up vibe

push the sky away
lady, come sing us in blue
the blues of loss and salvation

baby, you've got a snow-white coat
with blue-red stripes

In the village a drizzle rushes through the alleyways
chasing the mist away, flinging the rain aside.
With a shyness that does not dissipate, the jacarandas hide
a purple diamond among their branches.
You are four years old, the two of us tap-tapping along. Suddenly
as if opening the eyelids of time you ask –
was God ever a kid? and your voice licks at my hand

ah, we fly on a millimeter of time
the whole yearning,
wafting like a wind,
whirling
hold, let me hold you
don't slip away

* *

once the word was an ear of corn
was a body
was
a girl running in a field innocent of words

* *

like gamblers addicted to the light,
drunken skies
tossed on tiles. illuminated
like sparklers,
you are revealed
as one who touched
the sublime
now
the void

the one with no name

o g-d

imagine voiding yourself: visibly absent.
no presence no sign. nothing. all shuttered.
the house, the green leaning against the wall, glowing pale.
one way or
another, white recedes into darkness. no deep-down eruption.
celestial bodies hide their shame. the eye
weaned –
will continue to forget. no image. body. form. Nothing will
be there.
outside, a body imagines a fetal position – head folded into knees.
here the belly, touch here, touch,
the placenta remembers.
but pain finds you
whistling: woeeee! here's another.
now the void gets an address.
whirling back and forth
the lap lost.
the rest is only text in a book.

lacerations from an unsent letter

it happened amidst the aquamarine,

— why the sky,
what's the point in morning breeze

  if she's running, stealing into sun in no time,
  the softness of flesh betrays

  — woe to all angels, take caution with
       a slaughtering knife.

  me?

I'm left holding up a paper mirror glass,
   reflecting this tumultuous destiny

 …while the Love… lord… you didn't dare touch that.

   stars resembled holes
   punched by G-d

she crosses over the garden
   spotting a hue
     between daffodil and lemon
     looking at her

stubborn, rocking the cradle of time

the house watches and knows:

all happy families are unhappy
in their own way

we are the words
the music
the thing itself when you're revealed

can you even believe it?

penury

who pulled on the crimson bond of blood,
random,
just like that
without asking the name
merely withdrawing
the heavens
hiding
the world
vanishing

on a moonless night

wrapped in a baby blanket,
a moment sank into the lap of time
sealed by a kiss.
on high, a feather-cloud scrawled:
love your life
never will there be a moment like the moment before

oh my god,

this split
between her and life
her and me
me
you – you
and
your absence
are things that scare speech

sub rosa

how did you become a celestial body
age-old impossible
to cure

* *

Lord, the apple of your eye throbs unrestrained

torso

finito la commedia

A bird will scream tonight – Pierrot proclaims –
knitting her a quick eyelashed cage.
He cuts across the stage, crumples into the deepest of irises,
tinctures of shadow. Behind a tear, the mouth ocular
in perfect contortion, smiles in folds of green,
yellow of sleeves, smiles fuchsia in the weave
of a waistcoat.
Pierrot cackles:
A bird will scream tonight
Finito la commedia

torso

…cutting it from the mother's body
sitting on a pumice stone,
…cutting it out of arms gathered softly over the belly,
inclining to shelter his head
which is missing.
I watch her
not in dark speeches
not in sight
face to face
in a mirror.

breath

You can't know what you know until knowledge
collapses, the heart alone
the face washed away
wrestling with an angel
choking for air

lonely planet

Cry oh earth, oh pretty child, beyond the western edge
lies un-land, between the gates of Helios,
aside a paling rock –
she lies in a pocket of stars, kiss-close
from dream lagoon,
kiss-close to a river bleeding painfully,
where Lethe's delta drags lazy legs. They say
Acheron flows downward, slow
as forgetfulness. Minnows flash redolent eyes
while Venus, crimson-caped, wallows in auric feathers.
Hermes, winged in sandals, devours road-scraps
to darkened shores, devours them whole.
Hushed by heartbeat is their spangled gossip,
soothed by dock leaves
and mellow mulberries. But you –
so distant –
where are you? Why the ebbing labyrinth
with no one
to ask? Orpheus touched down, glanced back.
Away was I and so were you, turning

and perhaps

it didn't happen
you said,
you said is this the nothingness?
the unmarked territory?
the endless further?
if so –
it's surely moving

twist

there's no death, she said.
the spirit doesn't die, is not born.
the sternum, a cage
of ribs, life before and after, all is one.
she paced a pace away
she paused:
no point in looking for the twist
in which sunflower becomes sun

* *

I searched far, teetering on despair, daunted by distance,
(no one said if *there* is up or down) –

yes, I know what I find is not what I lost,
but must remember
not to let the light
drift between my fingers

roaming

Every night darkness types a cry. One only. Come –
every morning east wanders west, pulling you
by the heart. Roaming, you are sketched
along a thin vein
abandoning the secret of high tide at low
where all yearning flows toward me, not the sea.

the purple rose of tel aviv

facing a groaning wind

Something in the softness asks for a hand. Fate
wants to touch the way a finger removes dust.
You're a desperate bullet unloading its baggage –
let the cry burn without anodyne, without
magic, until the storm un-ends.
Hurricane stupefaction hits

but no,

we did not talk. Time fled down an alleyway.
The mouth blackened in a gnawing night.
From outside, there were no words. None.
Only talk of after. Night severed muteness
with a knife until it succumbed –
seventy silences burned

words steeped in weakness

Moving like an arrow. Clenched for takeoff.
The hand writes words steeped in weakness.
Answering the body.
Naming the unnameable. Mute within words. The ink blanches.

They throw a mumbling glance
…Is this art or a shred of life ripped away?

* *

Be seated. Be silent.
Let her scatter your blood, the fine lines
of your face. Let her be the feather that flutters
your heart, free within and out, from speech
or silence. Let the bitter rise on the slopes of sunrise mount.
Let the taste of storm
awaken

que sera

I didn't want to tell, but in the nest of your eye I saw
yellow-nippled lemons that made the sun blush
while teeny-weeny you, splashed with laughter and breeze,
swirled and swung, unmuted as others approached –

now you sing
                – que sera sera – as once I sung

run, the words do not clench around you
only beauty adheres

at daybreak I'll release you to dawn.

letsgo

pain, hold my hand, pain, letsgo
quick, we'll rinse rock salt from waves.
you're water, foam – frayed at the edges,
music in the viola neck of a cello,
crumb of dream between lips of void –
come, rest your head in my lap, close your eyes, hush.
we'll dream into being the purple rose of tel aviv
streaming onward
the river nevermore

Lightning Source UK Ltd.
Milton Keynes UK
UKHW011433161021
392324UK00001B/49